D1683264

03/11/2020
WOODS BRANCH
GROSSE POINTE PUBLIC LIBRARY
GROSSE POINTE, MI 48236

ZION WILLIAMSON

BASKETBALL SUPERSTAR

BY RYAN WILLIAMSON

Copyright © 2019 by Press Room Editions. All rights reserved. No part of this book may be used or reproduced in any manner whatsoever, including internet usage, without written permission from the copyright owner, except in the case of brief quotations embodied in critical articles and reviews.

First Edition
First Printing, 2019

Book design by Jake Nordby
Cover design by Jake Nordby
Photographs ©: Kyodo/AP Images, cover, 1, back cover; Streeter Lecka/Getty Images Sport/Getty Images, 4, 6, 18, 22; Kevin Ruck/Shutterstock Images, 8; Tracy Glantz/The State/TNS/Tribune News Service/Getty Images, 11; Kevin C. Cox/Getty Images Sport/Getty Images, 12; Jaylynn Nash/Icon Sportswire/Getty Images, 14; Brian Utesch/Icon Sportswire/Getty Images, 17; Red Line Editorial, 20–21 (infographic), 29; Lance King/Getty Images Sport/Getty Images, 20, 20–21 (Zion Williamson), 21 (left), 21 (middle), 21 (right); Rob Carr/Getty Images Sport/Getty Images, 25; Mark Lennihan/AP Images, 26; Patrick Semansky/AP Images, 30

Press Box Books, an imprint of Press Room Editions.

Library of Congress Control Number: 2019942523

ISBN
978-1-63494-141-9 (library bound)
978-1-63494-142-6 (paperback)
978-1-63494-143-3 (epub)
978-1-63494-144-0 (hosted ebook)

Distributed by North Star Editions, Inc.
2297 Waters Drive
Mendota Heights, MN 55120
www.northstareditions.com

Printed in the United States of America

About the Author
Ryan Williamson is a sportswriter based in the Minneapolis–Saint Paul area. His articles have appeared in various publications across the United States.

TABLE OF CONTENTS

CHAPTER 1
Beating the Heels 5

CHAPTER 2
Starring at a Young Age 9

CHAPTER 3
Meeting Expectations 15

CHAPTER 4
March and Beyond 23

Timeline • 28
At-a-Glance • 30
Glossary • 31
To Learn More • 32
Index • 32

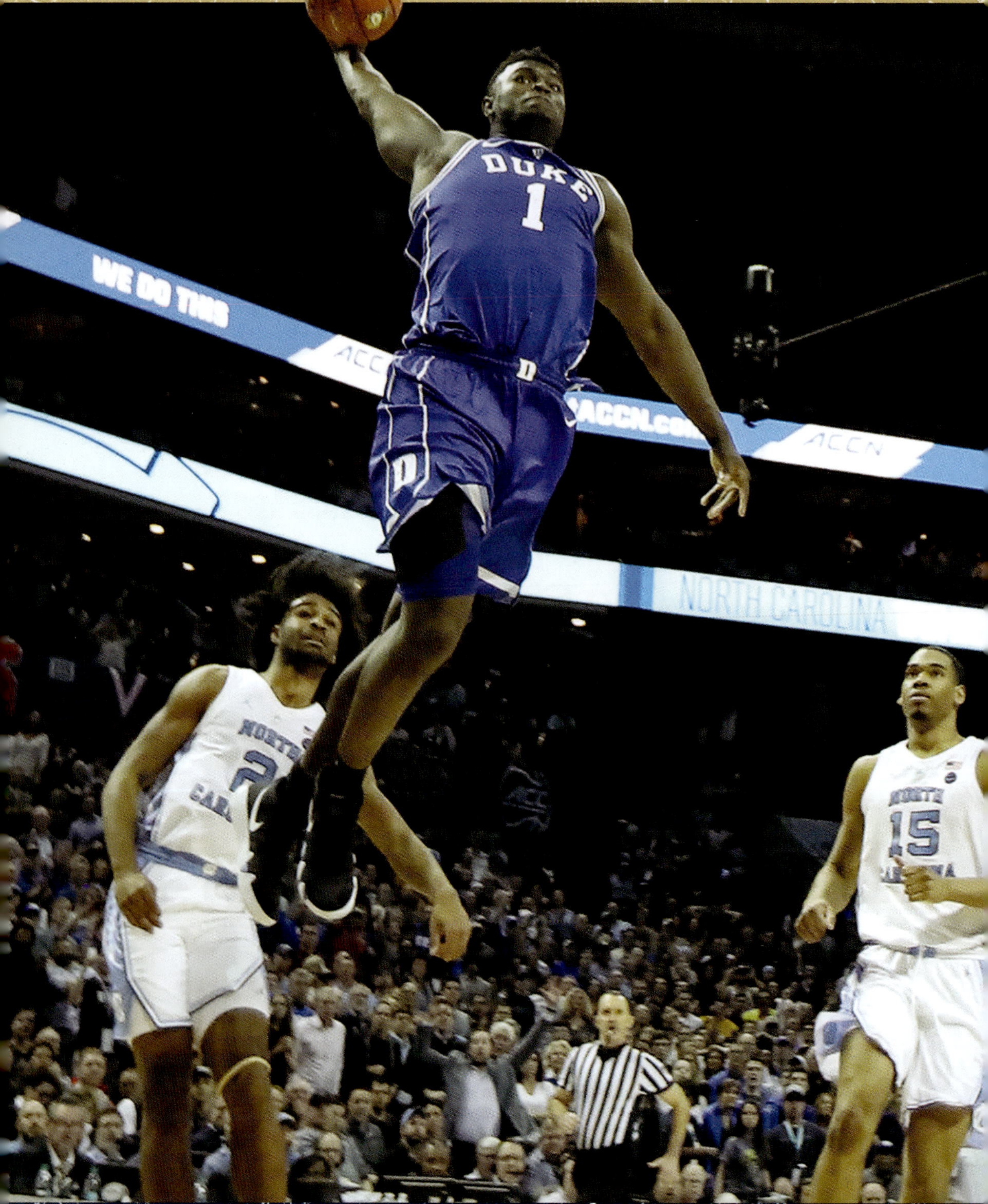
DUKE
1
WE DO THIS
ACCN
NORTH CAROLINA
NORTH
15

1 BEATING THE HEELS

The North Carolina Tar Heels were just trying to set up their offense. But Zion Williamson had other ideas.

The Duke Blue Devils forward stepped in front of a Tar Heel pass and took off the other way. Williamson was all alone as he threw down a one-handed dunk. He yelled to pump up the crowd. The fans roared.

Duke's rivalry with North Carolina dates back to 1920. Less than 10 miles (16 km) separate the schools. Any game between

Zion Williamson throws it down against North Carolina.

Williamson did some of his best work close to the basket against the Tar Heels.

them is a big deal. But this March 2019 game was one of the biggest. No. 5 Duke featured Williamson and two other highly skilled freshmen. Only the third-ranked Tar Heels stood in the way of Duke reaching the Atlantic Coast Conference (ACC) tournament title game.

The score was close throughout the second half. North Carolina led 73-72 with 35 seconds left. Williamson put up a short shot with a defender in his face. The ball bounced off the rim. Players from both teams fought for the rebound. Williamson outjumped them all and grabbed the ball. Then he tipped it back toward the hoop. This time, it went in.

Williamson's shot gave Duke the lead. The Blue Devils held on to defeat their rivals 74-73. One of the sport's brightest stars came up big when it mattered most.

FOLLOWING IT UP

The day after beating North Carolina, Duke played in the ACC tournament final against Florida State. Williamson scored a game-high 21 points as Duke won 73-63 to claim the title. Williamson was named the tournament's Most Valuable Player (MVP) for his performance.

WALL
STREET

2 STARRING AT A YOUNG AGE

Zion Williamson was born in Salisbury, North Carolina, on July 6, 2000. His mother named him after Mount Zion. That is a famous mountain in the Middle East. His family moved to Florence, South Carolina, when he was two years old.

Zion began to play organized basketball at age five. He dreamed of becoming a professional basketball player. He woke up at 5:00 every morning to work out. His family supported his efforts. His mother, Sharonda Sampson, coached his

Zion went to high school in Spartanburg, South Carolina.

youth and middle school basketball teams. His stepfather, Lee Anderson, helped him practice. Anderson had played college basketball at Clemson.

In eighth grade, Zion stood 5 feet 9 inches tall. He played point guard for his school and summer league teams. Then, in the summer before ninth grade, he grew five inches. He began playing forward. And his family moved to Spartanburg, South Carolina.

Zion started on the varsity team as a freshman at Spartanburg Day School. By his sophomore year, he was almost 6 feet 6 inches tall. He was already a talented dunker. He could also play point guard. Not many players his size could do both.

Once Zion started dunking in games as a sophomore in high school, people took notice.

Zion became a force in the middle for Spartanburg Day School.

Videos of his dunks went viral. NBA players talked about how impressive the dunks were.

By his senior season, Zion was one of the nation's top recruits. Spartanburg Day was

Zion shows off his moves at a McDonald's All-American Game event in 2018.

a small school. Some people wondered if Zion would leave for a bigger school so he could play with other star players. But he stayed at Spartanburg Day and had a strong senior season.

During his senior year, some college coaches had concerns about Zion's weight. His muscular frame carried 250 pounds (113 kg). The coaches worried his weight would keep him from being athletic enough to succeed in college.

But those concerns didn't keep schools from wanting him to play for them. More than 25 schools offered him scholarships, including Clemson, where Zion's stepfather had played. Zion committed to Duke during his senior year.

EARNING NATIONAL ATTENTION

Zion attracted attention from celebrities and professional athletes while in high school. NBA players Damian Lillard and Andrew Wiggins came to watch one of his Amateur Athletic Union (AAU) games. Rapper Drake and star football player Odell Beckham Jr. each posted a photo of themselves sporting Zion's high school jersey on Instagram.

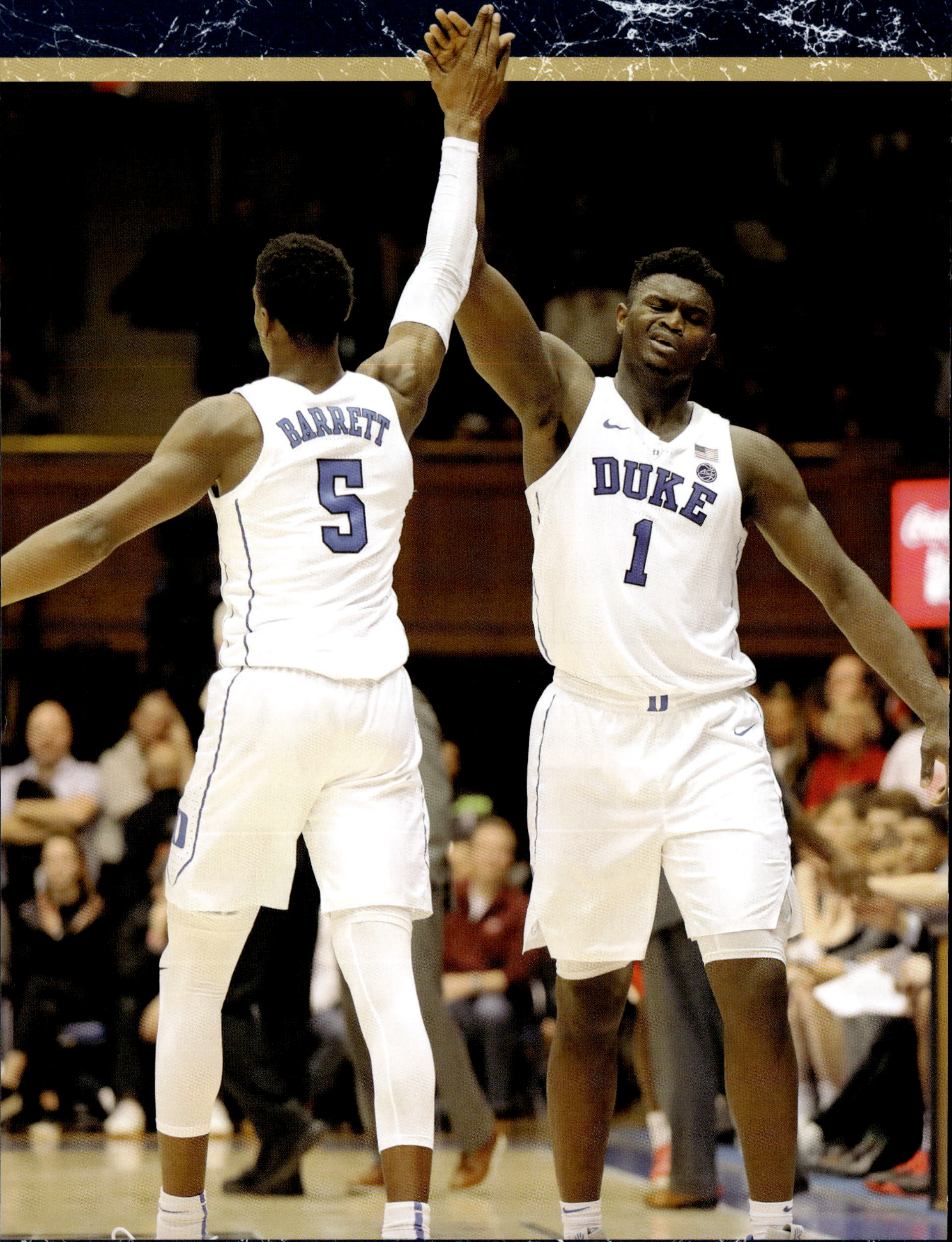
BARRETT
5
DUKE
1

3 MEETING EXPECTATIONS

Expectations run high in the Duke men's basketball program. But the 2018–19 season was special because Duke had three of the top freshmen in the country.

When the season began, Zion Williamson wasn't even the highest-rated recruit on his team. His dunk videos on YouTube made him the most famous freshman on campus. But RJ Barrett, a forward from Canada, was the top-ranked recruit out of high school. Cam Reddish, a

RJ Barrett and Williamson were two of the top freshmen players in the nation in 2018–19.

forward from suburban Philadelphia, rounded out the talented trio. He ranked just behind Barrett and Williamson.

Duke began the season ranked No. 4 in the nation. In their first game, the Blue Devils faced a huge test against second-ranked Kentucky. The Blue Devils put on a show for a sellout crowd in Indianapolis. Williamson showed his athletic ability with amazing dunks. He finished with 28 points as Duke blew out Kentucky 118–84. The Blue Devils showed they were capable of knocking off the nation's best.

As the season went on, Williamson continued to display his remarkable skills. He scored 35 points against Syracuse. That set a school record for points in a game by a freshman. He went viral after he jumped and spun around completely before dunking

Williamson became an instant fan favorite with his powerful dunks.

on a fast break against Clemson. Later that season, Williamson raced out from near the basket to block a three-point attempt from the corner. That move came in a big game against conference rival Virginia.

Williamson winces in pain after his left foot tore through his shoe against North Carolina.

Duke quickly took over the top spot in the rankings on the way to a 23-2 start. Then on February 20, the Blue Devils faced their biggest rival, No. 8 North Carolina. The atmosphere at Duke's Cameron Indoor Stadium was electric. Even former US president Barack Obama attended the game.

But the excitement that had built for the big game almost immediately turned to disappointment. Just 36 seconds into the game, Williamson tried to quickly change directions. He planted his foot. The sole of his shoe stuck to the ground. But his foot tore through the front of the shoe. Williamson injured his knee. He had to leave the game. Duke lost 88–72 without him.

A SHOE MALFUNCTION

Williamson's injury caused controversy. Nike, the shoe's manufacturer, was heavily criticized. But others blamed Williamson for wearing a shoe that wasn't made for bigger players. People also debated whether Williamson should keep playing after he recovered. Some thought the risk of injury wasn't worth risking his NBA future.

POWER AND GRACE

Zion Williamson is known for his ferocious dunks. One of his most famous came on January 5, 2019, in a game against Clemson. Williamson stole the ball at midcourt and raced to the hoop. With nobody in his way, he decided to give the fans a little extra for their money. He did a complete 360, spinning in a full circle, before throwing down a powerful left-handed dunk.

21

ACC BASKETBALL
CHAMPIONS
2019
NEW YORK LIFE ACC TOURNAMENT
CHAMPIONS
ACC

4 MARCH AND BEYOND

Zion Williamson did not play again in the regular season for Duke. But he still won the ACC's Player of the Year award. He averaged 21.6 points, 8.8 rebounds, and 1.8 blocks per game. He returned to the floor in the ACC tournament.

Williamson looked better than ever. In his first game back, he made all 13 of his shots and scored 29 points in a win against Syracuse. Then the Blue Devils knocked off North Carolina, getting

Barrett and Williamson celebrate Duke's ACC tournament championship.

revenge for two regular-season losses to the Tar Heels. Finally, they beat Florida State to win the ACC tournament title.

The Blue Devils entered the NCAA tournament as the No. 1 seed in the East region. Duke was a popular pick to win it all. But it was a tough road for the Blue Devils. They had an easy win in the first round against North Dakota State. But then Duke had its hands full with a tough Central Florida team. Williamson scored 32 points and grabbed 11 rebounds as Duke held on to win 77–76.

In the Sweet 16, Duke pulled out another close win against Virginia Tech. Up next was Michigan State in the regional final. Williamson scored a game-high 24 points. But the Blue Devils suffered a heartbreaking 68–67 loss. Duke came up one game short of the

Despite Williamson's best efforts, Duke couldn't hold off Michigan State.

Final Four. Even so, Williamson still had much to celebrate. He earned a number of national player of the year awards.

Williamson then had to decide whether to stay at Duke or enter the NBA Draft. It was an easy decision. He declared for the draft

Williamson got used to being the center of attention as he prepared for the NBA Draft.

on April 15. His one year with the Blue Devils had proven to be one of the most memorable seasons in college basketball history.

Heading into the draft, most experts thought Williamson would be the top pick. On May 14, the New Orleans Pelicans got the first overall pick in the NBA Draft Lottery. The speculation soon began over whether the Pelicans would take Williamson or trade the pick.

In the end, the Pelicans held on to it and chose Williamson with the first pick of the 2019 NBA Draft. He was joining a team that had just traded its biggest star, center Anthony Davis. Williamson would be one of six new players—including two other first-round picks—who were key parts of the Pelicans' rebuilding plans.

Williamson said he was excited to move to New Orleans and get to work with his new teammates. And on draft night, he had one simple message for the Pelicans' fans: "Let's dance."

THE ZION CAM

Once the NCAA tournament began, all eyes were on Williamson. Fans wanted to see what he could do in the biggest moments of his college career. CBS capitalized on the opportunity by rolling out the "Zion Cam" for Duke's games. This camera followed only Williamson whenever he was on the court.

TIMELINE

1. **Salisbury, North Carolina (July 6, 2000)**
   Zion Williamson is born.

2. **Spartanburg, South Carolina (2015)**
   Zion begins playing on the varsity basketball team as a freshman in high school.

3. **Atlanta, Georgia (March 28, 2018)**
   Zion plays in the McDonald's All-American Game, featuring the top high school players in the country.

4. **Durham, North Carolina (2018)**
   Williamson begins his freshman year of college playing for the Duke Blue Devils.

5. **Indianapolis, Indiana (November 6, 2018)**
   Williamson scores 28 points in his first collegiate game as Duke defeats Kentucky 118–84.

6. **Charlotte, North Carolina (March 14, 2019)**
   Williamson returns to the court for Duke after suffering a knee injury earlier in the season.

7. **Washington, DC (March 31, 2019)**
   Williamson plays his final college game. Duke loses to Michigan State in the NCAA tournament to end its season.

8. **New Orleans, Louisiana (June 21, 2019)**
   Williamson is introduced to fans and the media one day after being selected No. 1 overall by the New Orleans Pelicans in the NBA Draft.

MAP

AT-A-GLANCE

Birth date: July 6, 2000

Birthplace: Salisbury, North Carolina

Position: Forward

Shoots: Left

Size: 6 feet 7 inches, 285 pounds

Current team: New Orleans Pelicans (2019-)

Past teams: Duke Blue Devils (2018-19), Spartanburg Day School (2015-18)

Major awards: ACC Player of the Year (2018-19), Associated Press National Player of the Year (2018-19), Naismith Award (2018-19), ACC Tournament MVP (2019), John R. Wooden Award (2018-19)

Accurate through the 2018-19 season.

GLOSSARY

draft
An event that allows teams to choose new players coming into the league.

fast break
A play in which a team advances the ball up the floor quickly.

freshman
A first-year student.

point guard
The player on a basketball team who runs the team's offense.

ranking
A team's position in a list of the top teams voted on by a certain group, such as coaches or the media.

recruit
An athlete who college teams are interested in.

rival
An opposing player or team that brings out the greatest emotion from fans and players.

seed
A team's ranking heading into a tournament.

varsity
The top team in a sport at a high school.

TO LEARN MORE

Books

Glave, Tom. *Mike Krzyzewski and the Duke Blue Devils*. Minneapolis: Abdo Publishing, 2019.

Omoth, Tyler. *College Basketball's Championship*. North Mankato, MN: Capstone Press, 2018.

Williamson, Ryan. *College Basketball Hot Streaks*. Mankato, MN: The Child's World, 2019.

Websites

Duke Blue Devils Men's Basketball
http://www.goduke.com/SportSelect.dbml?DB_OEM_ID=4200&SPID=1845&SPSID=22724&KEY=

Williamson's College Basketball Recruiting Profile
http://www.espn.com/college-sports/basketball/recruiting/player/news/_/id/215742/zion-williamson

Williamson's College Stats
https://www.sports-reference.com/cbb/players/zion-williamson-1.html

INDEX

Anderson, Lee, 10

Barrett, RJ, 15–16
Beckham, Odell, 13

Drake, 13
Duke Blue Devils, 5–7, 13, 15–19, 23–27

Lillard, Damian, 13

NBA Draft, 25–27
NCAA tournament, 24–25, 27
New Orleans Pelicans, 26–27
Nike, 19

Obama, Barack, 19

Reddish, Cam, 15–16

Sampson, Sharonda, 9

Wiggins, Andrew, 13